MW00985912

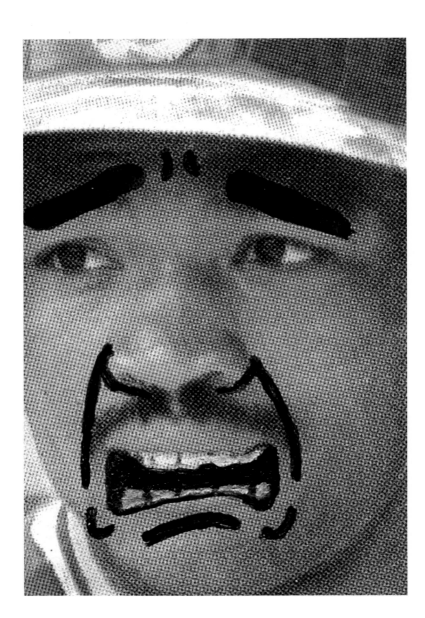

"THAT'S MESSED UP."

—Harold Reynolds, discussing Baseball Card Vandals on MLB Network

BEAU & BRYAN ABBOTT

CHRONICLE BOOKS

SAN FRANCISCO

First published in the United States of America in 2019
by Chronicle Books LLC

Library of Congress Cataloging-in-Publication Data available.
ISBN 978-1-4521-7360-3

Manufactured in China.

Design by Spencer Vandergrift

Chronicle Books LLC
680 Second Street
San Francisco, CA 94107
www.chroniclebooks.com

10 9 8 7 6 5 4 3 2 1

CONTENTS

WHAT THE EFF IS BASEBALL CARD VANDALS?

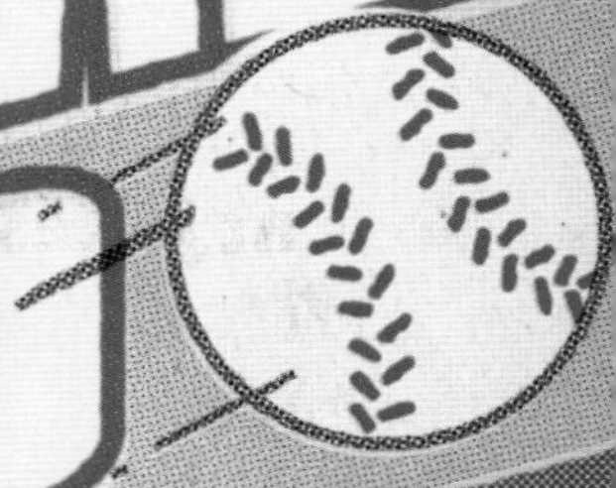

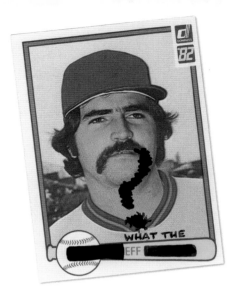

WHAT THE
EFF

Decent jokes on worthless cards, posted fresh daily.

This was the mission statement dreamed up by two brothers, Beau and Bryan Abbott, when we began a project called Baseball Card Vandals back in 2012. As a pair of artistically inclined baseball nerds, we were honestly just trying to entertain ourselves and maybe some friends by scribbling crude jokes on our old baseball cards. In the years since our first Tumblr post in 2012, that mission hasn't really changed at all. Everything else in our lives, though—transformed by the strange power of Sharpies, old cardboard

and the glorious people of the internet—has changed completely. And to understand how Baseball Card Vandals went from a hobby to a website to a business to the book you're holding, you have to know how it all started: an obsession with baseball cards.

We grew up in the late 80s and early 90s in the suburbs of baseball-mad St. Louis and learned quickly from our older brothers Ben and Braden (yes, we're all Bs) that the best way to blow all of our allowance money was to turn every last cent of it into baseball cards. This became a hard-and-fast rule that also extended to any bonus money acquired from birthday gifts, visits from Nana, or some other invented scheme to generate capital

BEAU - CHRISTMAS 1995

BRYAN - 1995 Christmas

TWO YOUNG VANDALS. AS YOU CAN SEE, WE REALLY LIKED KEN GRIFFEY, JR. AND THE BEASTIE BOYS. WE ALSO HAD A WEIRD CAT WALL HANGING.

(like Bryan's inspired idea of telling adults that he was "collecting current U.S. coins.")

Saving money for something that cost more than $5 or was made out of something other than cardboard? Whatever. We wanted the thrill of opening the pack; the curatorial authority of sorting the "good" from the "bad"; the naked idolatry of putting a Ken Griffey, Jr. rookie card in a "plastic" to display and adore and protect as if it were the key to our salvation; the prestige of having an awe-inspiring yet somehow never complete collection of Rickey Hendersons (Beau) or Darryl Strawberrys (Bryan).

For our younger selves, money was baseball cards. Actual dollars and cents were just the tools necessary to acquire our sacred currency: Topps, Fleer, Donruss, Score and Upper Deck (and later Stadium Club, Ultra, Bowman, Pinnacle and even Triple Play). Baseball was our religion, and baseball cards had photos of the hairy gods on the front and glorious hymns written in numeric code on the back. Bryan was convinced that if heaven really was a magical place in the sky, then surely there must be a mint condition Darryl Strawberry 1983 Topps Traded on every damn cloud.

Now this obsession may seem a little pathetic, but the joys of baseball card collecting were true and plentiful. To this day we believe, without any proof whatsoever, that our collections helped build our unique identities and sense of selfhood, and that the design, photography, and graphics on cards helped foster an aesthetic sensibility that led to our lifelong interest in art. Or something like that.

But our obsession also carried with it two unfortunate by-products. First, it taught us that saving money was just plain stupid, because we wanted new cards every damn week. Secondly, we became straight-up hoarders, with boxes and binders of cards filling our closets and the space under the bunk bed and most of the floor of our shared bedroom, the majority of which were the bad cards, or "commons," sorted away from the charmed and magnificent good ones which went straight into plastics and binders.

Unfortunately there was nothing that could be done about our practiced aversion to saving money (it's still very much with us). We were able, however, to put that massive supply of common cards to creative use during the countless unsupervised hours that kids with working, divorced parents are given. Inspired by the Fun Cards submissions published in the Beckett price guides, we picked up our Sharpies and started scribbling crude jokes all over our most pathetic cards

in endless attempts at entertaining one another. We drew fart clouds, ginormous penises, caricatures of TV stars, players screaming cuss words, gruesome injuries . . . the predictable silliness that rattles in the mind of young smartasses poured out of our Sharpies onto our most pathetic cards. Whatever this hobby was, we did it frequently and competitively enough that we got pretty good at it. And since our only audience was each other, we quickly developed a sort of shared comedic language that stayed with us and (thankfully) evolved as we got older.

And thus the seeds were planted. During those lazy afternoons of sitting around submerged in stacks of worthless cards and permanent markers, with *Saved by the Bell* or *Family Matters* flickering noisy nonsense in the background, with the Ken Griffey, Jr.'s and Frank Thomas's safely sheathed in plastic and carefully situated in their Right Place, and with absolutely nothing else to do, two brothers with no prior criminal records became Baseball Card Vandals.

Well, kinda. That's not the whole story. There's a big gap, after all, between two kids killing time after school drawing on their Dickie Thons and Don Aases, and two grown men running a business selling marked-up commons. How'd we get from there to here?

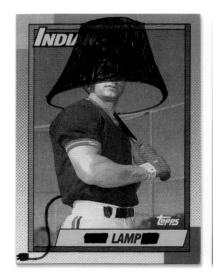

OUR FIRST BIG TUMBLR HITS, "LAMP" AND "I IRON EACH OUTFIT."

As we "matured" into "adults with real jobs," we had some ideas for creative projects we wanted to work on together. Our main focus was creating a T-shirt brand. We wanted to take our love and knowledge of baseball, mix it with our artistic sensibilities, and create a line of unlicensed MLB shirts that were cooler than anything else on the market. We spent a few months working on designs, drawing our favorite players, and conceptualizing weird team logos and apparel. Once we had a decent idea of our plan, we took a week of vacation from work to finalize designs.

Of course, each night after the "serious" work of disrupting the T-shirt industry was completed, we sat around until 4 a.m. drawing on cards. And by the end of the week, we had a six inch tall stack of defaced '86, '87, and '90 Topps with a few Score, Donruss and Fleer cards shuffled in. They were pretty damn funny, and unlike the still-imaginary T-shirts, they were done. To create an apparel company, we still needed a bunch of money, an e-commerce site, an ownable look and feel—there was a long way to go. But these cards were finished, they were funny, they were nostalgic, crude, hand-drawn—exactly our aesthetic. So one night in late November, we decided to start a Tumblr, mostly for the instant gratification of seeing our ridiculous drawings up on the internet. At the very least, it would be something to play around with while we got our shirt shit together.

We uploaded the first card, "Hungover," a very primitive BCV piece that relies almost entirely on the player's miserable facial expression and profuse sweating. We called the blog Baseball Card Vandals and decided to post two cards a day, one drawn by each of us. It wasn't perfect, but it was ours. And for better or worse it was now live for the whole Internet to see.

Shockingly, our weird artwork immediately found an eager audience. And in the years since we launched, we've continued to draw, post, and (eventually) sell completely bonkers cards every single day—over 4,000 published to date. It's a true labor of love and at this point we honestly just don't know how to stop.

As the Baseball Card Vandals on the Internet, we hope to make you smile a few times a day. This book was put together with that same spirit. If you're already a BCV fan, first of all, we love you. Thanks for helping us finally do something with our lives for once in our, um, lives. We hope you enjoy this collection of old hits and new cards created exclusively for the book.

And if you're not a fan of BCV . . . we apologize in advance for what you're about to see.

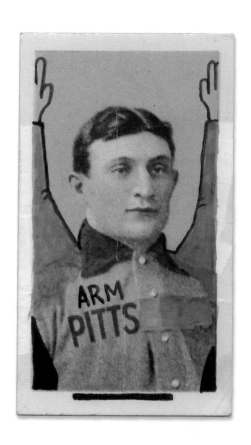

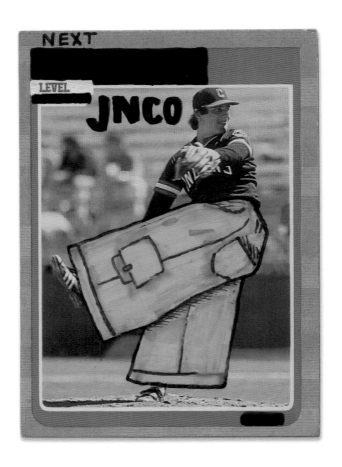

ALL STARE

WE

AT WIRELESS PHONES

19

FEEDING ████
APPLE JACKS ████ TO

MARINE ████

LIFE...

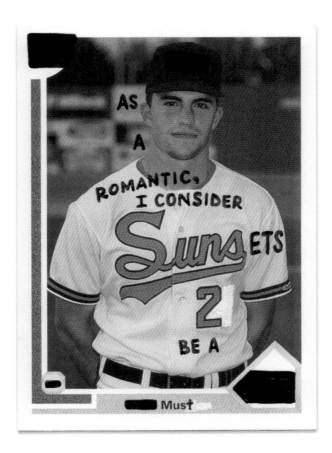

AS A ROMANTIC, I CONSIDER SUNSETS BE A

Must

21

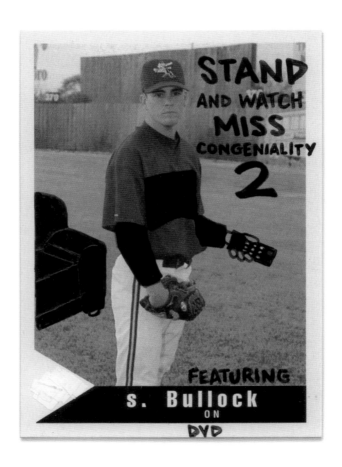

STAND AND WATCH MISS CONGENIALITY 2

FEATURING

s. Bullock

ON

DVD

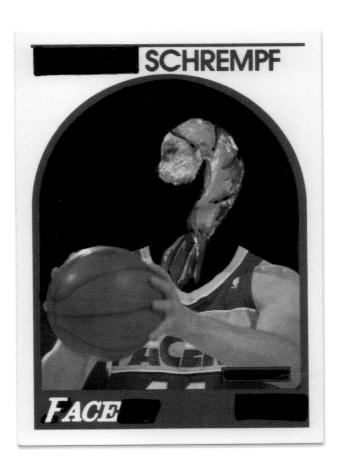

SCHREMPF

FACE

BLESS

Dis

HOUSE

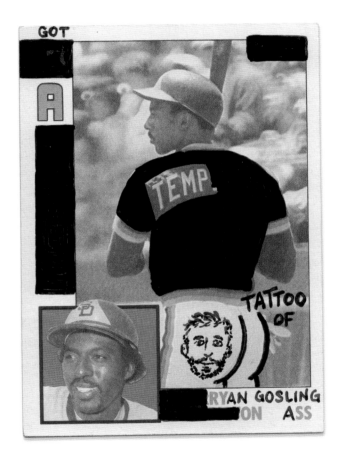

31

PLEASE BE THE

Phil

TO MY COLLINS

V. VAN GO

BEEN A LONG **TIME** SINCE I HAD MY

WOODY HELD

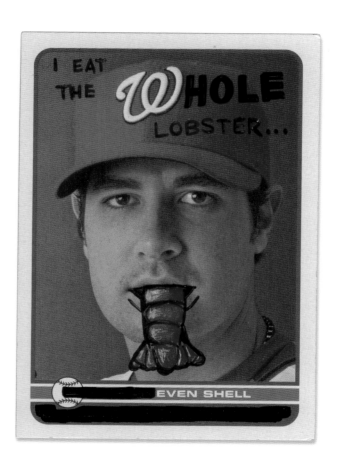

I EAT THE WHOLE LOBSTER... EVEN SHELL

QUEEN

F ROG

sex

SET MY **VCR** TO

RECORD   EACH

Monk   Season

39

odd

NEIGHBOR

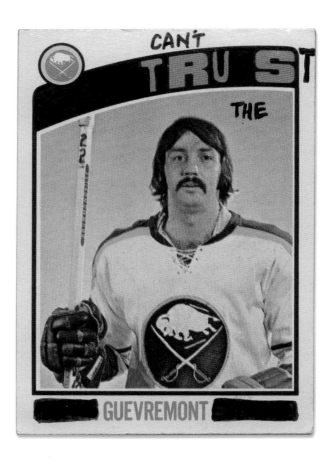

CAN'T TRUST THE

GUEVREMONT

43

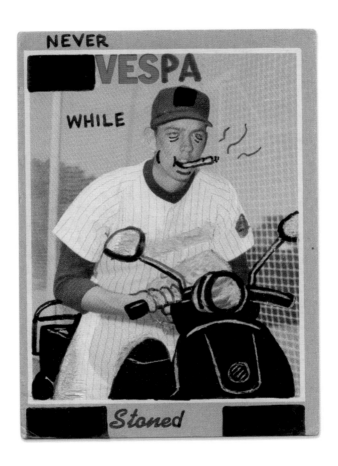

WOOD

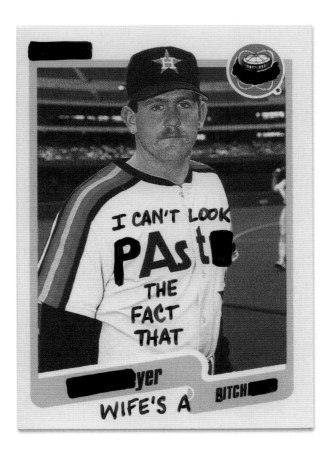

Will Clark KENT

EVER LET HIS

GIANT

SECRET OUT?

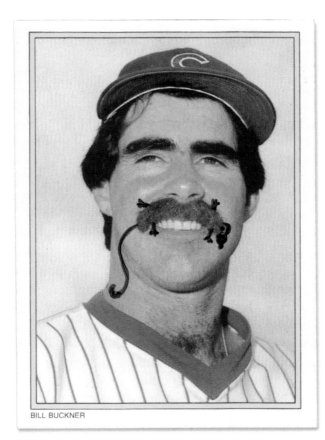

BILL BUCKNER

POP
TART

HIGH LIFE OVER

REG MILLER

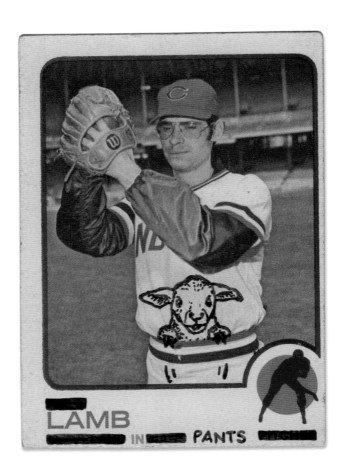

LAMB IN PANTS

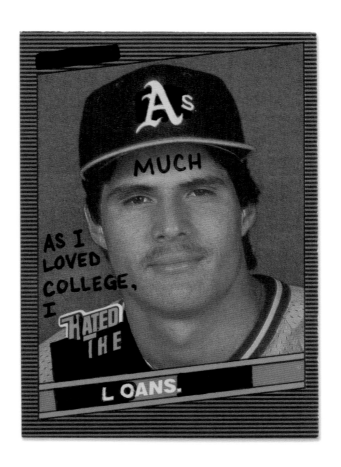

MUCH

AS I
LOVED
COLLEGE,
I HATED
THE

L OANS.

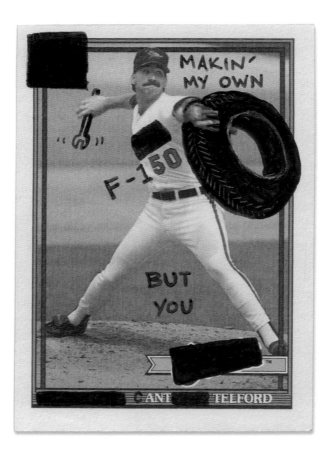

FRAMED A
PICTURE
AND

SPENT A
FORTUNE

on Matting

SIT

ON DURHAM

STREAKER

PLEASE STICK TO
DA█ RIVERS
AND
DA
LAKE█S
THAT YOU'RE USED TO...

THE SHITTING AREA

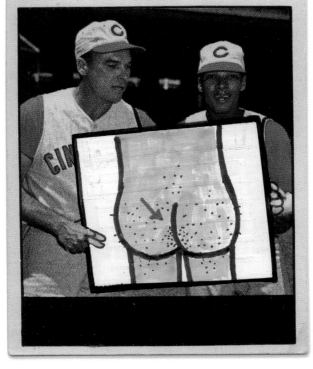

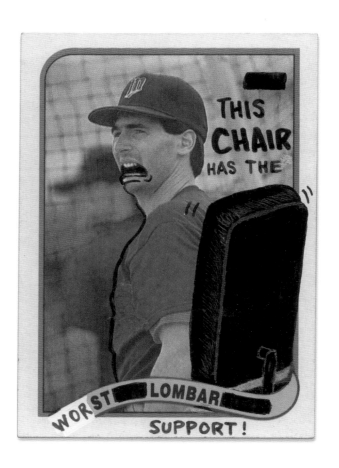

THIS CHAIR HAS THE "" WORST LOMBAR SUPPORT!

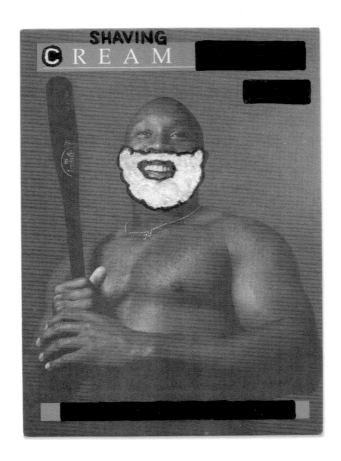

SAY

ANYTHING

I HIDE MY ANGER

AND LIVE

A ██████ LIE

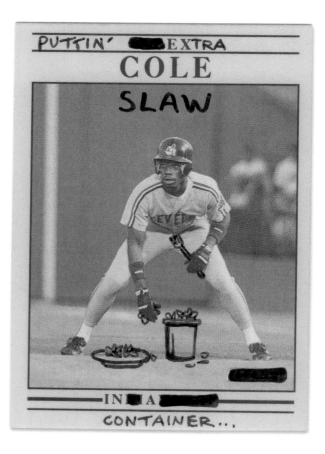

PUTTIN' ███ EXTRA
COLE
SLAW

IN ██ A ████

CONTAINER...

69

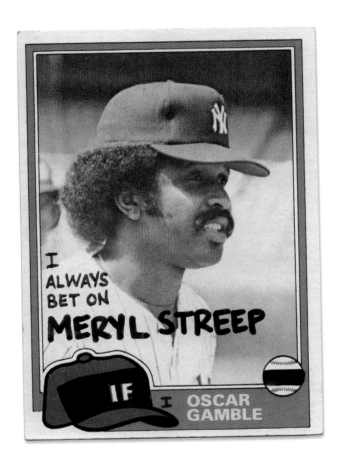

71

FRAME

HOLDER

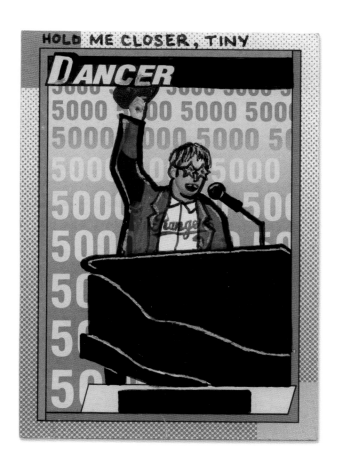

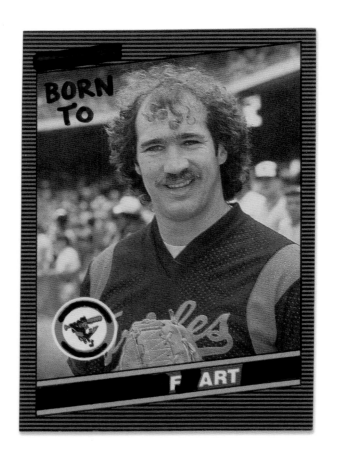

BORN TO

F ART

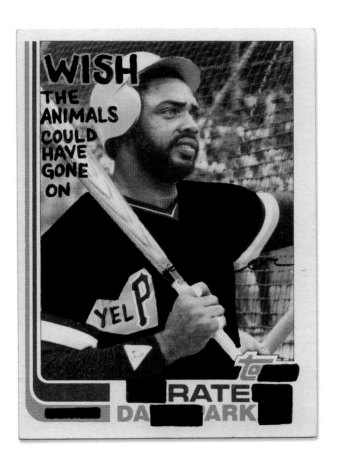

79

TEEN WOLF

WITH

MICHAEL J FOX

81

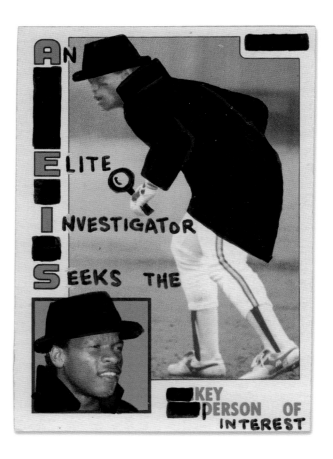

AN ELITE INVESTIGATOR SEEKS THE KEY PERSON OF INTEREST

WOOKIE
STAR

CHUBBEKKA

LEFT MY CHAPSTICK IN
THE ▮▮▮ DRYER...

THE WORLD WIDE
WEBB

GAS
NOzzle S

SHE ALWAYS
ATE DRY
TOAST 'TIL
I

INTRODUCED

HER

TO BUTTERS

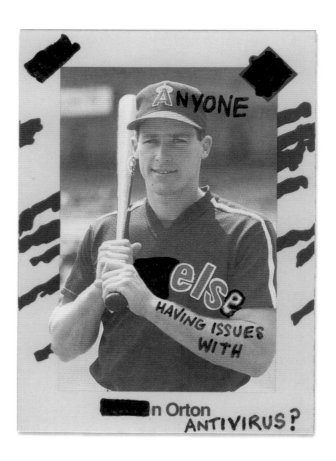

ANYONE

else

HAVING ISSUES
WITH

█████n Orton

ANTIVIRUS?

BEARD

FACE COAT

90

I QUIT CHILI'S ▮▮▮ WHEN OLIVE ▮▮▮ GARDENHIRED ME A$ Mgr. ▮▮▮▮▮

91

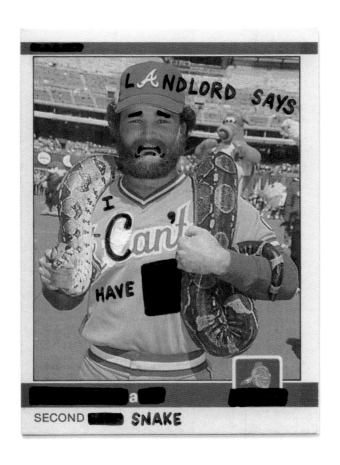

SECOND ███ SNAKE

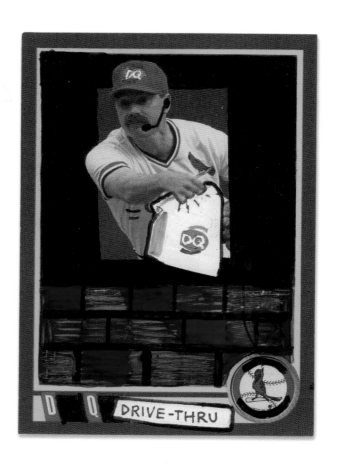

DRIVE-THRU

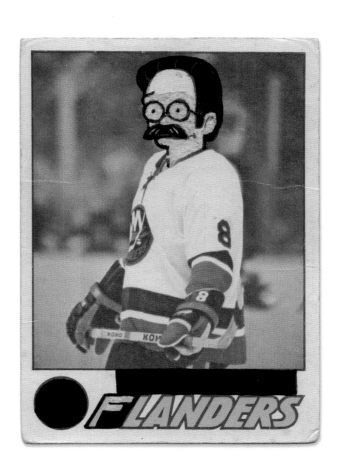

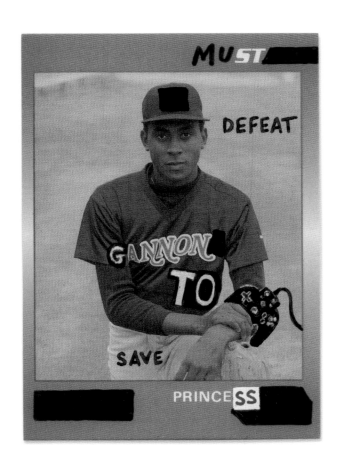

SOLLY

A TRULY DOPE

MC WILL

JUST EAT

THE

MICROPHONE

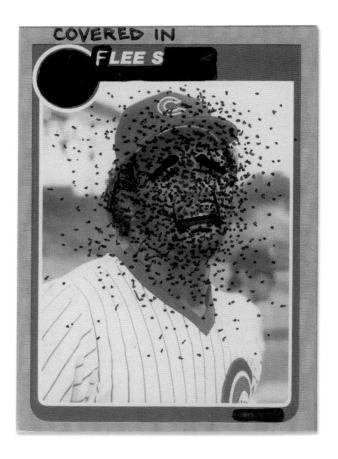

COVERED IN
FLEE S

PUTTIN'
MY ██████ SNOW CONE

ON ██████
INSTAGRAMS

101

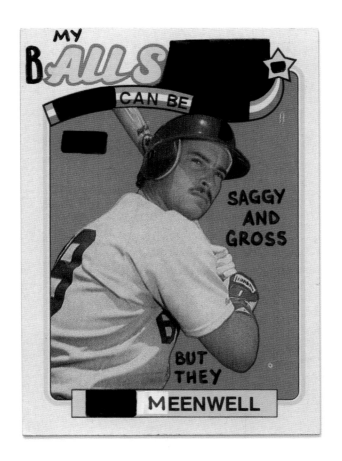

MY

BALLS

CAN BE

SAGGY
AND
GROSS

BUT
THEY

MEENWELL

103

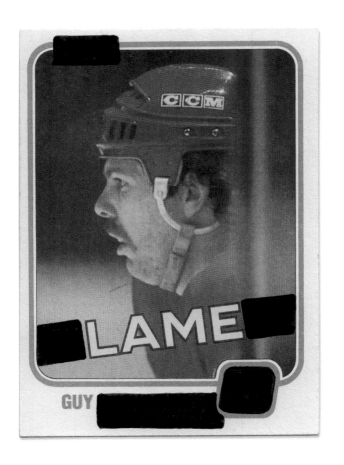

LAME

GUY

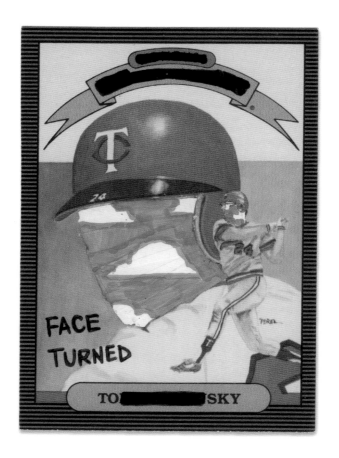

CARL WINSLOW

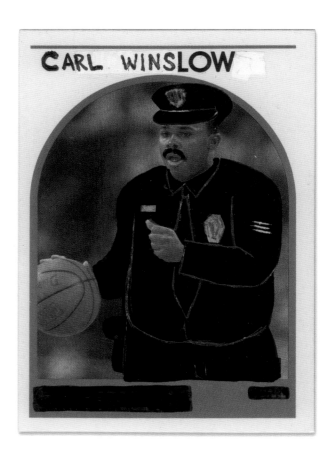

THE FERTILE CRESCENT BETWEEN THE TIGRIS AND EUPHRATES WAS THE CRADLE OF CIVILIZATION

109

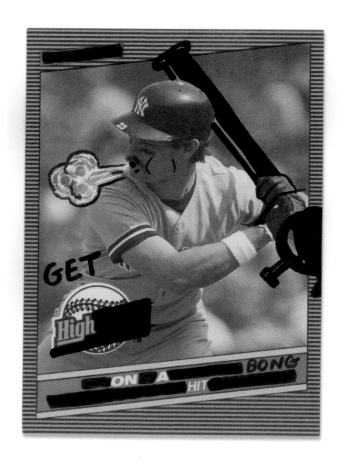

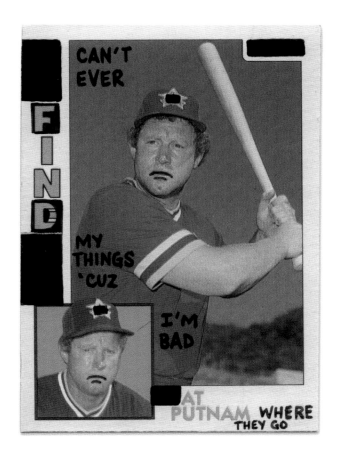

CAN'T EVER

FIND

MY THINGS 'CUZ

I'M BAD

AT PUTNAM WHERE THEY GO

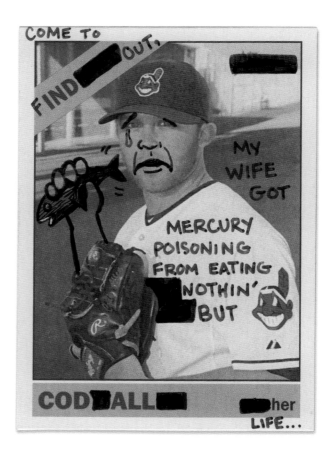

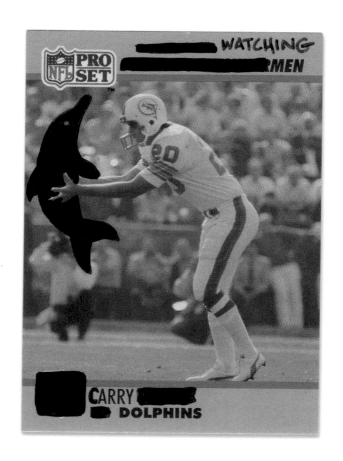

WATCHING � ████████ ████████████ RMEN

PRO SET NFL TM

CARRY ████████
DOLPHINS

STONEHENGE

THE

BEST

COAT
FACTORY

BURLINGTON

117

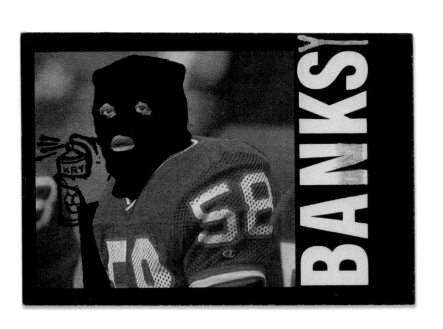

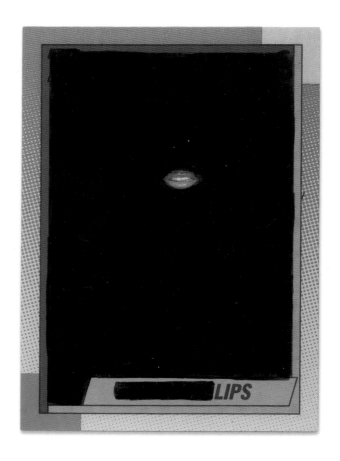

LIPS

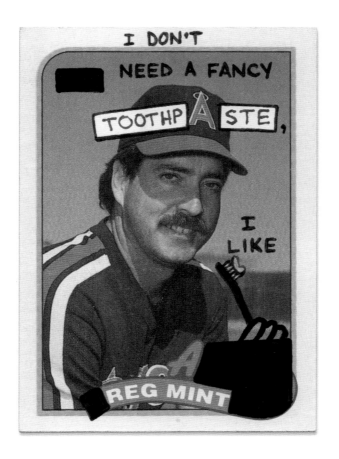

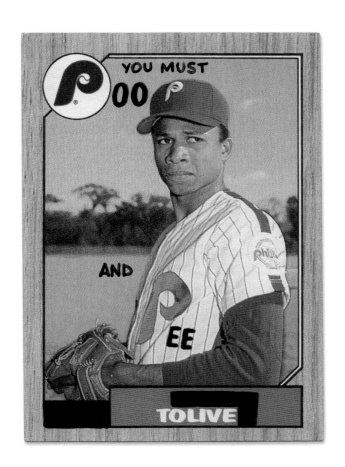

YOU MUST

00

AND

EE

TOLIVE

123

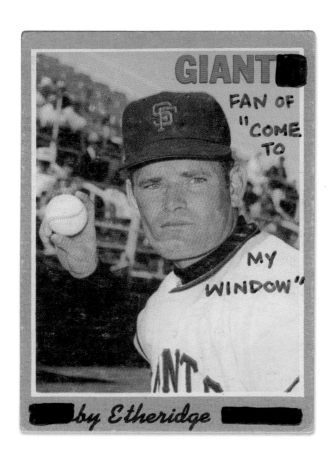

GIANT

FAN OF "COME TO

MY WINDOW"

by Etheridge

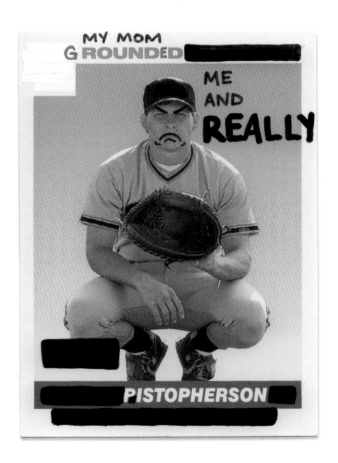

MY MOM
G ROUNDED
ME
AND
REALLY

PISTOPHERSON

125

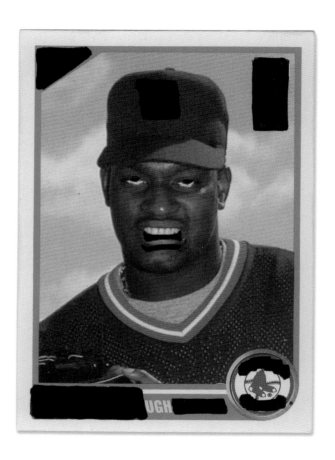

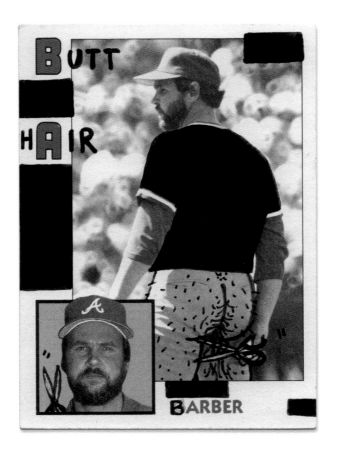

BUTT HAIR

BARBER

127

HOTEL

LOBBY

128

WATCHING TITANIC HOPING THAT KATE WILL

EFF LEONARD

129

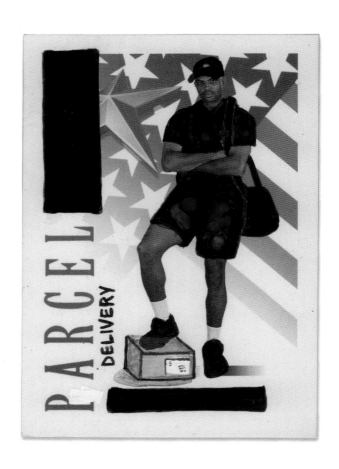

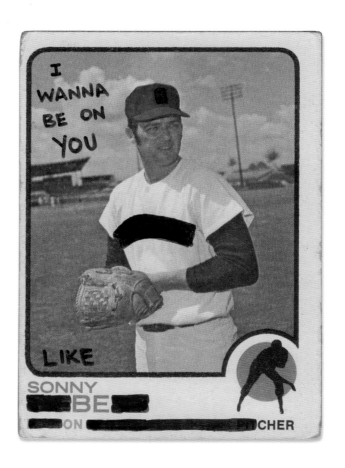

PEARS

IF YOU CAN'T HANDLE ME AT MY **RINGO,** YOU DON'T DESERVE ME AT LENNON

139

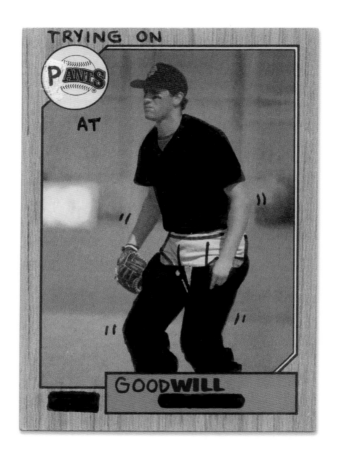

FEET

141

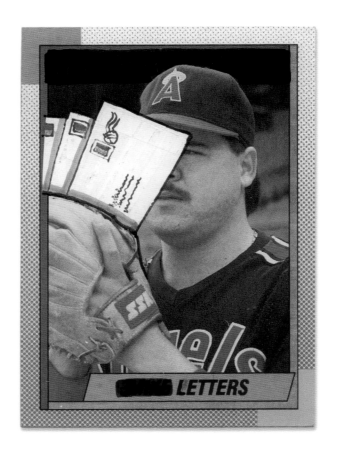

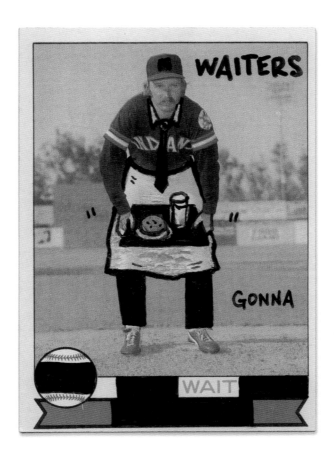

STUCK *in* A LADDER

147

MAKE LIKE A TREE 'N LEAVE

TOLD MY

DANG

BOSS

IKE WITT

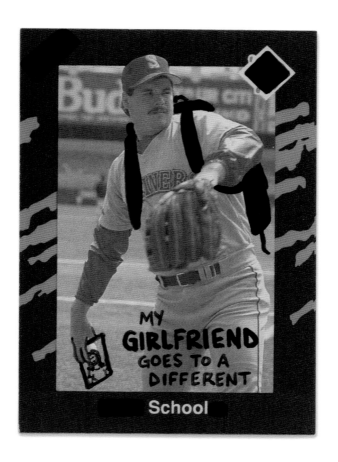

MY
GIRLFRIEND
GOES TO A
DIFFERENT
School

151

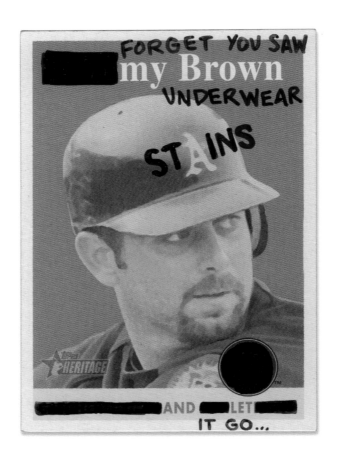

FORGET YOU SAW my Brown UNDERWEAR STAINS

AND LET IT GO...

152

DRAKE

153

155

LINT
ROLLERS

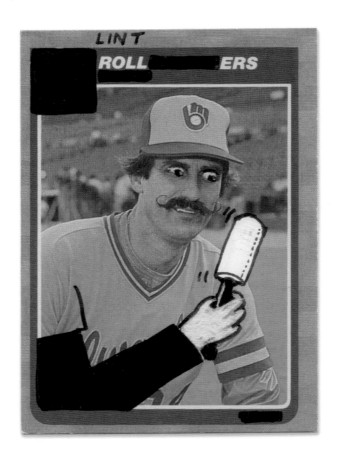

WITH THAT ASS, I DON'T KNOW HOW YOUR

PANTS MANAGE

157

JUST LIKE

a ladden

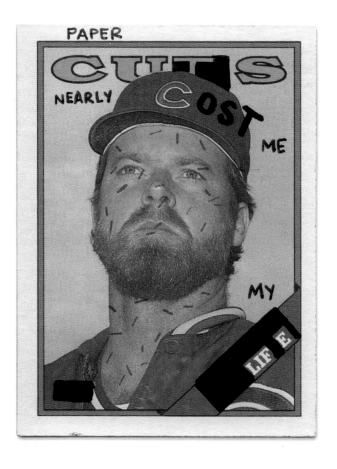

159

WOULD YOU LIKE

ANNY
SANGRIA?

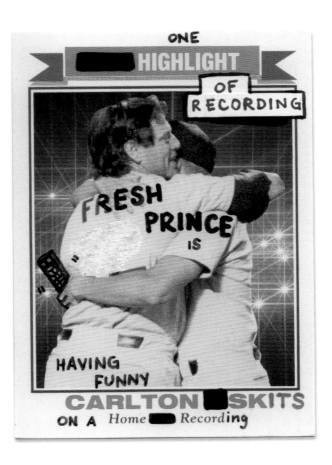

ONE ██████ HIGHLIGHT OF RECORDING

FRESH PRINCE IS HAVING FUNNY CARLTON ██ SKITS ON A Home ██ Recording

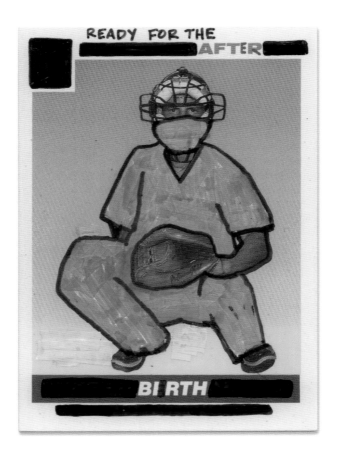

SCRAP BOOKING IS A

HAPPY CRAFT

163

ROSS CHERISHED

RACHEL

MORE

THAN YOU THINK

166

THE
RED
PLANET:

Mar S

STUCK IN

A

DANG
BANNISTER

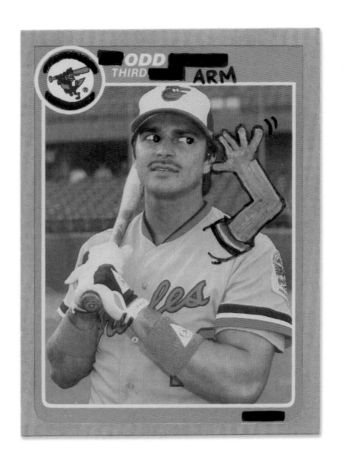

ODD
THIRD ARM

172

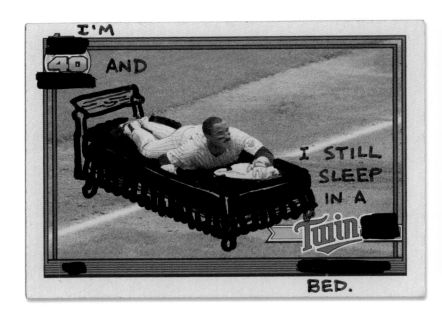

174

YOU CAN'T ██ BEAT ██ THESE

marine ██ THEMED PANTS...

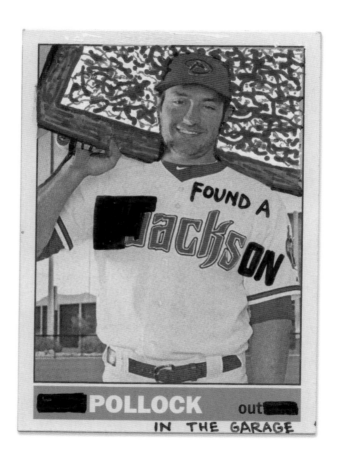

FOUND A

Jackson

POLLOCK out

IN THE GARAGE

BRUNCH

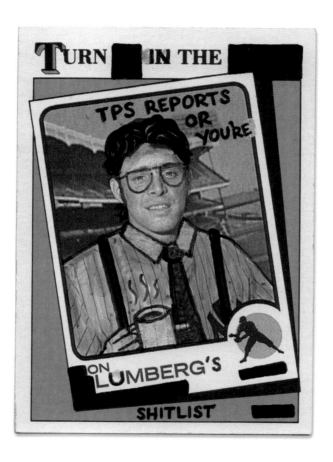

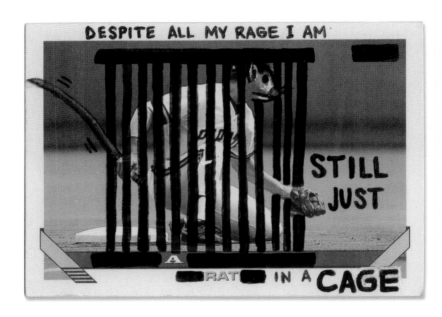

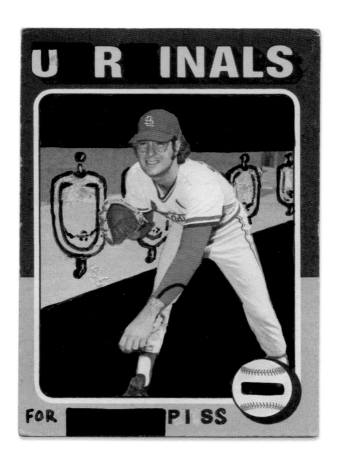

183

CHERISH

A BURP

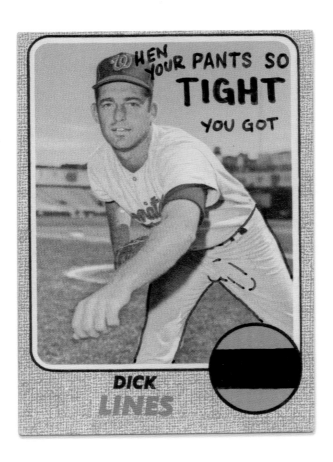

DROPPIN' A FEW

CUPS

OF

CHUNKY BUTT
RAIN

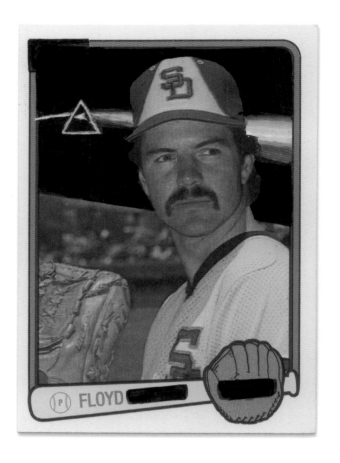

(P) FLOYD

189

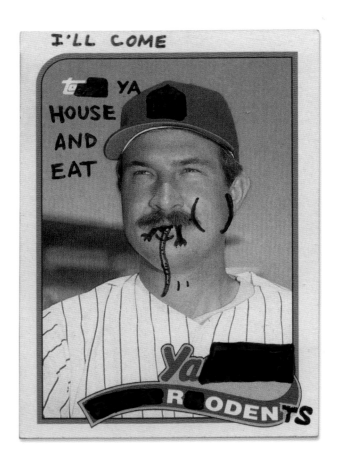

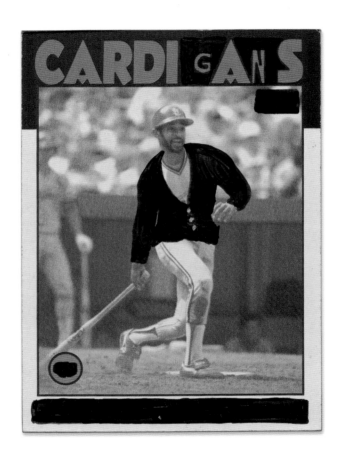

WAYNE
SIMPSON

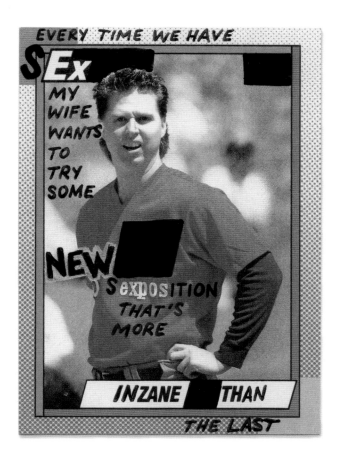

EVERY TIME WE HAVE S**Ex** MY WIFE WANTS TO TRY SOME **NEW** S exposition THAT'S MORE INZANE THAN THE LAST

PHARRELL

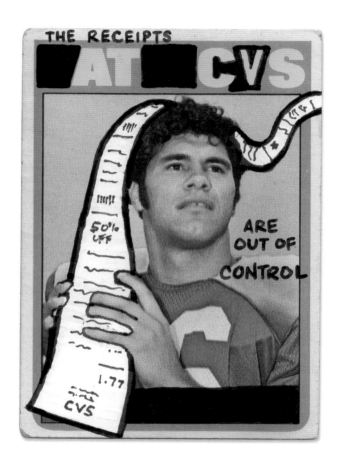

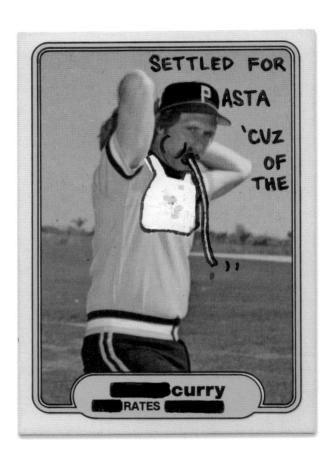

SETTLED FOR
PASTA
'CUZ
OF
THE
"

curry

RATES

SHADED

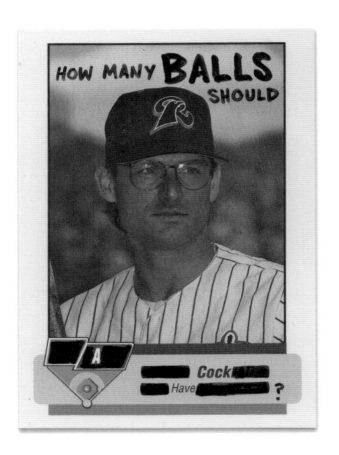

GOT ME A FRAMED BOY GEORGE POSTER OFF EBAY

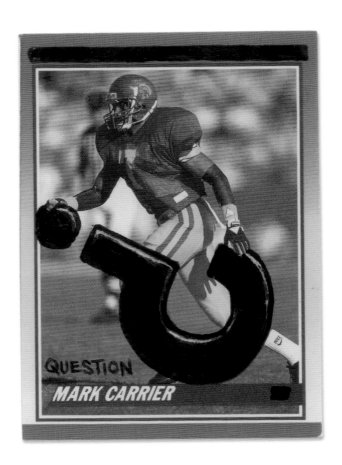

QUESTION

MARK CARRIER

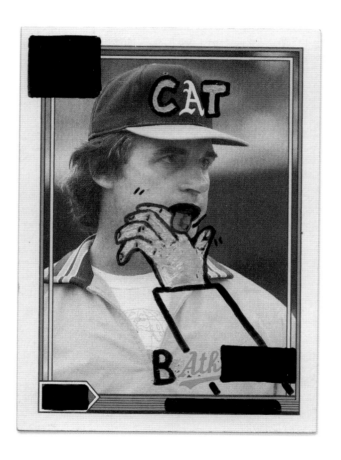

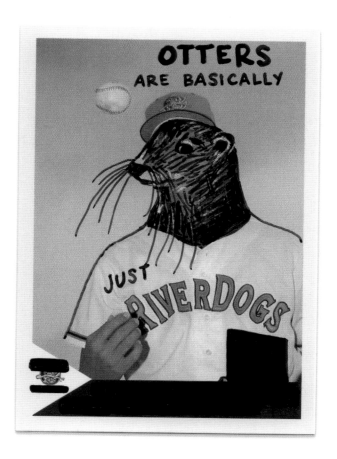

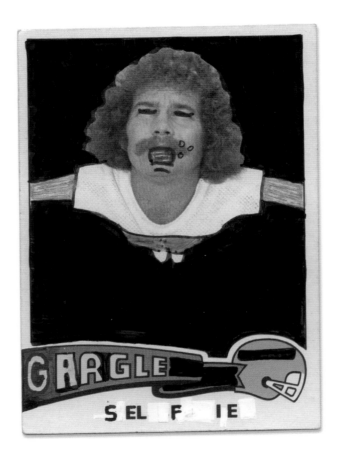

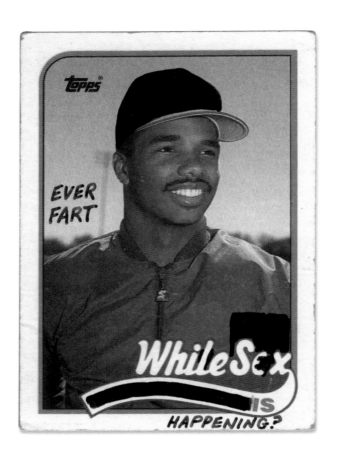

EVER
FART

WhileSex

HAPPENING?

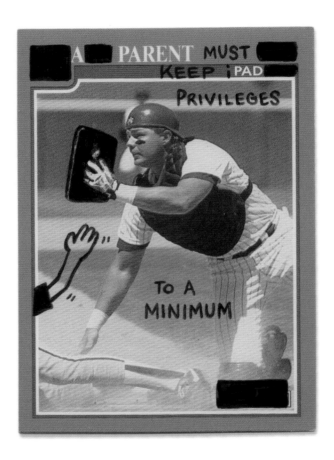

STEPS

211

N IGHTGUARD

BOOBS

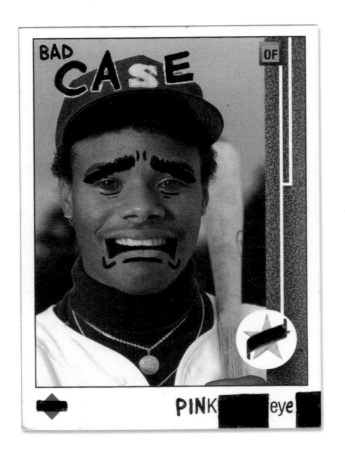

BUTT CHEEKS

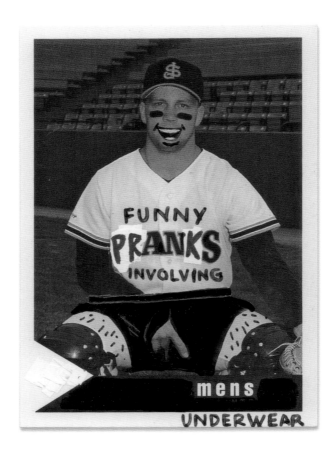

Acknowled

THERE ARE JUST SO MANY ~~DANG~~ THANK YOUS...

This book, and Baseball Card Vandals in general, simply wouldn't exist without the exuberant support of our family. We love you all and not a day goes by that we're not grateful to be Abbotts. To our brothers, Ben and Braden, thank you for showing us that dudes can be weird, cool and thoughtful at the same time. Following in your footsteps has given us a level of confidence in ourselves that wouldn't exist without your lead.

A huge thank you hug to the BCV Mom, Chery Curbow, who you may know from her Instagram comments. You always kept our house stocked with art supplies, our heads full of encouragement, and our hearts full of love. Plus, you always let it slide when we left a few Sharpie stains on the kitchen table.

Don Abbott, aka Pops, watching you laugh at our cards is one of our great pleasures in life. Thank you for encouraging us to be fearless and always throwing your support behind our ideas and passions. After all the books you've given us, it feels pretty great to give you this one.

To Nana, you are the shining example of why kids love their grandparents so much. Your kindness and generosity are endless, and we're so incredibly grateful to have spent all that time riding in your minivan.

And to Brittany: you've been subjected to more dumb BCV jokes and outlandish BCV dreams than anyone else on Earth, and that can't be easy. Thank you a million times for always indulging our absurdity, and for believing in our ability to turn it into something worthwhile. Your love, humor and help has meant everything. Plus, we'll never forget "Kirby" . . .

Thanks are also due to all the friends who laughed at this nonsense before it had a name, especially Evan Martoia, Hardeep Singh, Brent Steele,

218

Jeff Nowack, Keith Noah, and Micah Hutton. Shout out to William Mead for sending a link to our website to Yahoo! Sports way back in 2012, landing us our first press.

Thank you Matt Vasgersian and Harold Reynolds at MLB Network for giving us a few thrills on slow news days. Thanks to Marty Sartini Garner at Flood, Eitan Levine at Mashable, and Jack Moore at Buzzfeed for making us look like a real thing. Thanks to Josh Reddick and CJ Wilson for giving us some actual MLB cred. To John Gualdoni, Rachel McInnis, Norty Cohen, Matt O'Rourke, Zach Gallagher, Pete Favat, and Dana Commandatore: thanks for treating two inexperienced draft picks like Rated Rookies.

It's hard to know the best way to thank so many people we've never met, so we'll just offer our deepest gratitude to all our loving fans and patrons, including some of our most dedicated supporters: Matt Logelin, Sara Andress, DH Callahan, Joseph Ferree, Sam Hunt, Andrew Kuo, Graham Elliot, Kelly Koch, Michael Kalmbach, Joe Rowland, Darren Frayne, and Joshua Rotteveel. This book doesn't exist without the support of you all!

Rachel Sussman, thanks for taking the time to explain to us what a literary agent is, then showing us how it's done. A huge thank you to Rebecca Hunt and the entire team at Chronicle Books for making our book dreams come true.

And finally, to Topps, Donruss, Fleer, Score, and Upper Deck: thank you for taking all of our money as children, then letting us earn a little bit of it back as adults. Baseball cards forever.

About the
AUTHORS

BRYAN ABBOTT

Bryan is 2½ inches taller than Beau. He is a self-taught graphic designer who can also do masterful impressions of just about any Major Leaguer's batting stance. He currently works as an Art Director and lives in Los Angeles with his classy dog Milu.

BEAU ABBOTT

Beau is 2½ years older than Bryan. He holds a BFA in Painting & Drawing from the San Francisco Art Institute, as well as the distinguished title, "grad school dropout." He currently works as a copywriter and lives in Los Angeles with his wife Brittany and their crazy dog Benny.